# Trigger Warning /
# Author's Note

**Caution:** This book contains disturbing material
and subject matter. Try the Table of Contents.
Maybe poems from "Sirens of Olympia" or "Cas-
cadia." There are no guarantees. Perhaps open
the book to what you need to read right now. Or,
take the journey, as chartered, with me.

Read it in a safe space—the way in which it was
written.

I've never seen a Phoenix rise up out of the ashes;
but plenty of trees—
evergreens.

# April on Olympia

# April on Olympia

## Lorna Dee Cervantes

Marsh Hawk Press · 2021
East Rockaway, New York

Marsh Hawk books are published by Marsh Hawk Press, Inc.,
a not-for-profit corporation under section 501(c)3
United States Internal Revenue Code.

Cover photograph: Lauriel Amoroso
Cover design: Anna Reich

FIRST EDITION

Library of Congress Cataloging-in-Publication Data

Names: Cervantes, Lorna Dee, author.
Title: April on Olympia / Lorna Dee Cervantes.
Description: First edition. | East Rockaway, New York : Marsh Hawk Press,
2021.
Identifiers: LCCN 2021044624 | ISBN 9780996991261 (paperback)
Subjects: LCGFT: Poetry.
Classification: LCC PS3553.E79 A85 2021 | DDC 811/.54--dc23
LC record available at https://lccn.loc.gov/2021044624

Marsh Hawk Press
P.O. Box 206, East Rockaway, N.Y. 11518-0206
mheditor@marshhawkpress.org

*This is dedicated to the none I love.*

*Any resemblance to any person, living or dead, is purely hypothetical.*

# Acknowledgements

*Thank you to the publishers and editors of the following publications in which the following poems first appeared in their original of previous stages.*

*Xóchitl, In Cuícatl, 100 Years of ChicanX Poetry, 1920-2020*
"'What is XicanX?'," "It's Not The Tulips' Fault," and "The River Doesn't Want the Wall." (Spanish translations by Gabriella Gutiérrez y Muhs.)

*Puro Chicanx Writers of the 21st Century*
"'What is XicanX?'," "It's Not The Tulips' Fault," "Not A Poem For Francisco X. Alarcón Who Wanted A Love Poem On the Occasion of His Death," and "The River Doesn't Want The Wall."

*The BreakBeat Poets Volume 4: LatiNEXT.*
"Did You Hear What They Said?" and "Blood."

*Poetry of Resistance: A Multicultural Anthology in Response to Arizona SB 1070, Xenophobia and Injustice*
"Olmecan Eyes."

*Olympia Power and Light*
"Living Ectoplasm."

*WATER, WATER, EVERYWHERE (website)*
"Moldering Rocks Listen to Things."

*POETRY Magazine*
"'Night Magic (Blue Jester)'."

*Colorado Review*
"Dogwood (Two)."

*Thank you to the organizations (and their participants) who invited me to teach, in which some of these poems were seeded and flourished: VONA (Voices of Our Nations Arts Foundation), CantoMundo, and The Evergreen College, among others. Thank you to my past students for providing the prompts (titles) in the poems in "April in Olympia" and elsewhere. Thank you for NaPoWriMo, National Poetry Writing Month in April, again.*

*Grateful to all my fine friends (you know who you are) who helped to keep this poet housed and fed. This book's for you.*

*Grateful, especially for all the music, musicians, and venues: Rhythm & Rye in Olympia (RIP), Nectar Lounge, and The Blue Moon Tavern. Thank you to The Andy Coe Band: You helped keep me alive, literally. Thanks for the dance. Thank you to my musician brother, Stephen Cervantes. "Without music, life is simply stupid." — Friedrich Nietzsche*

*Thanks to trees. Without you, nothing would be possible.*

*The poet wishes to acknowledge and thank the following for the inspiration and use of quotes: Billie Holliday, Joni Mitchell, Art Garfunkel, Leonard Cohen, Robert Hass, Pablo Neruda, James Baldwin, Guillermo Portabales, "El Carretero," and Theodore Roethke.*

# Table of Contents

**Destination Anywhere**

**Sirens Of Olympia**

## Cascadia

*On Olympia*

## The River Doesn't Want the Wall

The river doesn't want The Wall.
It wants to ring free where it wants.
The river doesn't want The Wall.
It wants to roam through the home
of the brave. It wants to run free
with salmon, with stone, with ceremonies
older than borders. It wants to cross
with the swell and drain. Rain doesn't want
a wall to contain it, to constrain the span
of progress. River wants to merge its way
to confluence. River wants to mingle and feed.
River wants the rocks to sing freedom's song.
River wants Wind to speak its peace.
The river doesn't want The Wall.
The land won't let it. The floods
won't cede. The People will sing,
"The river wants to let freedom ring!"
The river wants to let my people go.

## Upon Hearing the News: The Hearing

I am more than the smell
of fear grasping my collar.
Not enough showers in the gas
chambers to assuage this stench.

I will cover you in silken
compassion; sheets of white
snow fall in this avalanche of absent
heart. Here is my heart, on the ground

at Wounded Knee. In this country,
hoods of white linen foil on me.
Mt. Hood in the glory crepuscular
distance, a distant memory of histories

of reprisals against us. You against us.
I never said this. "Where is your empathy?"
I say. Sunken subjugated knowledges fling
port off your "Fridge," ice cold in the Arctic

no matter who owns her.

# Radio Blues

Listening to Oliver North and the NRA,
the birds want blues 'though they'll jam
with Bird. They love the treble clef,
the skat falsettos. But there's nothing
that gets them going more than
B.B. King. The thrush dare
the drone. Some bird calls inquisitively
from the weedy thicket. The wave of Scotch
Broom crests in the logged lot next door.
They own the city 'scapes, crowding
and encroaching as is their ilk,
poisoning the earth around them,
spilling their seed willy nilly—families
of yellow bouffants and coifs upon the land,
feeding nothing; while Oliver North sells arms
there's a war upon the world. The birds
know, and vote for blues, again.

## Harbor Fest in Olympia

They're singing sea chanties on The Virginia V
at the precipice of the end of the new age.
A gray couple drives a blue tug with a rainbow flag.
The old tall ships are there for the fantasy.
What's another million to the handful of Squalxin
dancers? The steps and rhythm set the scene,
half-forgotten remnants—words of the slaughtered.
The daughters circle, circle-dancing the arc
of The Sun. Rainier melts in the near distance
forgetting its name, Tahoma. The Capitol
reflected in the algaed pond wilts
in the climate changed summer

All is well in Texas: a deep water.
Sodden hawks huddle
in open taxis. How many still dying...
an unasked question. The bayou
overflown, the tidy houses drowned.
5 million tons of refinery emissions
sting the eyes and lungs like livid
fighting fire-ants. This is how it is
in a post-nuclear age. When corporations
are considered people, the corporations
don't consider people.
The flooded homes bear their sad legacy
of trash and refuse. Day after day
Justice lags behind with Compassion.
The water wells as Spirit swells
and the hearts and bodies rise.

## For The Melting

How do you deport
the dead? Those wounded
soldiers under the cloak
of history? The histrionics
of race and class, the farce
of the better half (as if
the sea had parted), those left
thirsty in the dark, those left us
with no form of resuscitation
nor reason: reason with me.
Take a browning hand, and let go
the golden ark of motherhood.
May I excuse the feckless,
the devoid who void, and cancel
the heart of the matter? Only
for a dream of crossing over,
they dwell in the cell
of the earth. Of the dearly
departed, deported draining
drowned desiccant, a flounder
of freedom, of the under
class denomination; demeaning
and meaning. History will awake.

## Three Poems Mourning the Murder of Martin 50 Years Later

**You/Me/Them**

### You

I was three-fifths human
less for what I seemed
to lack. I was hunted
haunted by what was

I was

You for a time being
for the being in time
I was extinguished
terminated in my own land

I was

where you are standing now
part allegiance, part pure
memory. I was strung by sinews
for learning, dead for the lesson

I was

### Me

You

      were an animal
      in my given God's eyes
      we milked you, cattle
      chattel to a man

You

      weed to clear
      for my consumption
      you, less than
      the seed I bore you

You

    nothing but law
    lawless on your own turf
    I gave you your living
    what I took from your land


**Them**

I am

Justice, Earth eternal
Truth in planet mind
a changeling thing. A change,

I am.

## Poem For Black Lives Matter

> *"People are not what we say they are.*
> *People are more complex than that. If you*
> *think that's what people are, you get Washington,*
> *then you get that cretin in The White House...*
> *[based upon] economic arrangements of the Western world."*
> — James Baldwin, Feb. 1968

Love is a force
greater than fear
a presence

and a present
a prescience sense
a nuclear subatomic

fusion. Baldwin knew
the past is not exempt
nor empty

as the future
a looming no
thing—a hushing

Power is
as power does
we reap the centuries

Don't let the age
be a mask
a Soul on ice

They live
They lie
but not a life

bearing light
to each
their own

black hole:
a toroidal sphere
of Name

and promise
until Death
do not US part.

## Imagine

Imagine a world
where Freedom happens
Rainwater collects in the sorry
gutters of a land branded "America."

Imagine a universe
indivisible—ourselves
cells of a being larger
than our worlds. Imagine.

Imagine a peace
without end, an endless
journey, an occupation
without the preoccupation.

Imagine a project
of the art's content
each quenching drop
a vote for life.

Imagine a life
story for all.
Imagine the time
to stay and listen.

Imagine a world
where help happens
unobstructed at the river
of our states, united.

Imagine a self
sovereignty of our body's borders
Trust in the presence
no matter the matter.

Imagine a bridge
of humanity across the globe.
Rainwater collecting in the sorry
gutters of a home branded, "America."

## Olmecan Eyes

Olmecan eyes gaze into the future,
a path of light piercing the forest,
heavy-lidded with the past, ancient
sorrows carved into stone. With rain,
the present leaks into now, into the DNA
of fallen stars, the mystery of oceans,
the settled silt of settling into culture.

Into the history of obsidian blades,
a human heart beats on the plate,
the slate of our division thinning
into someone's blood. The blood of
The People surging still beneath
the pursed lips, the pierced tongue,
the sudden pulse. We are The People

still. Our constitution stolen
from us in the fear. We rise, not
vengeful, but full of the peace
of knowing, our present tense.

Olmecan eyes reborn. The infant
stone unfurling in our navels.
Another civilization reconquers
the wilderness of today. Sun devouring
Earth, we are shadows of the way
we were, beneath the shifting planets,
the comets, the desolate inconsolable moon.

# It's Not the Tulips' Fault

*For César Chávez & Angelica Guillén, in memorium*

It's not the tulips' fault
If a boy dies in the waiting room,
Penniless. It's not the fallen petals' fault
If a girl, caught in the migra's grasp,
Gets deflowered in the mud.
Don't blame these flagrant perfumed
Mouths. Their dumbed words would house
Horrors. If they could speak they would
Wonder at the work of man, the toil
Of this endless labor of making fortunes
Only to lose lives to the withering cells'
Demise. Don't blame the tulips
For their poisons, for the bees dying
At the pollen's promise. Don't make them
Suffer the pickers' thirst. They bare backs
To the riven sun striped and stripped
Of sustenance, their dried out tongues
Caught up in the moment of rich desire.
Once they were wealthy with color, with
The vibrant fluid of justice pooling in
The uneven fields. Once they were worth
More than a man, a single hardened heart
Worth more than ten women's bodies.
Once their fists of bulbs moved Earth,
Weighted heaven. Once they were more
Valuable than the dirt they languor in.
Once they were winter's bitch, holed
Up in their dank holes, waiting. Once
A hundred thousand dollar bills fluttered
Over the promise of these Purple Hearts,
These fiery red heads and yellow ribbons
Of silken hope. Once, an entire country
Lay in their immigrant wake, their green
Fingers poking at heaven like the devil's
Cock. Once an entire nation lay captive
At the feet of the harvest. Once, an entire
Nation was held captive and the earth
Beneath their feet stolen and pock-marked
With the quest for gold. Now, these stark

Blood tulips lie, a reminder, remainder,
The inflation of their fleshy bowls
Starving the people who harvest, who
Hunger at the work of tulips. 5 for a buck.
Five campesinos' lives per fistful.
Don't blame the tulips. It's not their fault.
Caught in the frozen clay of history, they will
Not obey. They are. These hearty gangs
Last a week, if that.... While brown backs toil,
While a child's armload weakens and
Death is forever. It's not the tulips' fault.
Give them a drink. Tell them what the sins
Of the fathers have sown. Vow now
Under the sun to end the suffering, to equalize
And organize: organ, eyes...
Organize. Organize! ORGANIZE!

## "What Is XicanX?"

To be XicanX is to be
a mongrel, half-breed, centipede
with a hundred avenues to bear;
To be XicanX is to cross the street
when either side arrives times quanta,
is to dodge the anyway and never have
a home; To be XicanX is to never speak,
never spoken to you swear on your
mother's side and then, besides your
*father was...* (and they decide your heritage);
To be XicanX is to take the risk:
exposure, suicide, an uncounted number...;
You maid around in an invisible suit;
You know the bite of dogs, threat of suits,
the laws—miscegenation applies to you,
who you love may not love you back; You take
The Paperbag Test and fail; You know how
to fold a bag, tie a knot in plastic; "Savage Wench"
is what they call you in the census books: to be
XicanX is to have no category, no one
that applies; To be XicanX
is to have a placenta in the ground over and over
in this Liberty one for all here: this world
"Between Two Waters," this America here,
over and over and over 'til the age
our ancestors first engraved upon the shells
of food now gone extinct (as we were once declared),
our mothers' names erased...; To be XicanX
is to be América, America, not a "race"
("...for I, too, am America!")
Sometimes I spell it with an X:
It means The People (and I birth)
in any language.

## Lemon Drop

We were up for anything, any role
our masks could carry off, our stands
on the street corners advertised well. Our
scuffed shoes and candied hands, our only sweet.

Dry as old lemon seeds, we "wild
women" told it off, all of it: the bone,
the stall, the match, the mall; the telling
made us taller, made men's lips pucker.

We, tight as the fists in our ready midst,
rattled in the gourd in rituals of tardy bells
and clinking pens gathered on our sills; the potent
seed, hidden within an acrid smoke.

We doled out the piled white, opened
vast the stolen taps. Our taps, silent
to our soldier's tasks. Our tapas, finished.
Two tarts on a roll. We never got a cent.

Our babies fell on broken streets like lemon
drops, sensuous, green. The lipstick blanched
our lips into fish to swim in those tight bowls
allotted us. US, a lot, our lot, to sell: For Sale.

## Until He Can Begin to Remember, I Delay, Gate The World, Learning Flow, Slow Remembering

Until he can begin to remember someone
shuts off the flow, the slow remembering
cracks the leather of his binding. All
the green given to cherish lay fallow
at his feet, a missed history test,
the stamping hooves behind the gate.
Before him, an expanse of what he'd been:
the freedom of the steady rain, now delay.

The corral begins slowly, a gate
constructed in the world, the horses follow.
Each splinter of wood splices beings,
a give and take of recollection. Gather
the would of world and all you have
left is weary. The flow stalled, the
still, a vast plain of forgotten...

## Evergreen

Evergreen clung to her hair, a depth
perception, her strung out red blurred
the vision, the great eating inside out.
She shot up vials of yellow sap,
the menthol fire of alcohol
in the mix, the fixing of future
in the passing of sense, the third
eye, a hole in her arm to the hip,
a swelling of lip and the crackling
of something foreign: the wildfire
taste of eucalyptus.

Magic happens in a needle, evergreen
medicine filling the air with cedar,
the bough that covers the runaway slave,
the branch that feeds the flame.
Evergreen forests with their memories
older than our own, we hold their ragged
hands in photographs that hung with dates:
the births and deaths of our voyages. Ever
green, the immense growing, sequoia
and scrub pine hug the depths, un abrazo
to the air, to what grows within.

## Inside An Hour

she was dead. Her halo hung in the starry
starry night. She had finally done it
this time. She was aware of the heat,
the hum of summer bugs, the trick
and trickles of sweat at the forehead,
the bangs she never foresaw. She
was a chalkboard for what he couldn't
hear. She was a heart stalled on a dare.
She thought she would live forever
inside an hour. Inside an hour
she was dead, a still oozing mush
and *must she?* Sixty times her beatings
cut in half. The thing she did to do
something. While men want
"something to be," she needed to do
to stop doing.

## After Julia Alvarez

I have something to say but the world pointed
otherwise. Dark-skinned palabras hung
at the bar. Sol y Tierra danced. Mi Nombre
just kept trying to warm up to The Sun. "Don't
confuse me with wit," la declamación de Los
Sueños declared, or the great forgetting; bottled
up and shaken: aposento, morivivi,
Las Mañanitas. Summoned as a tide
of island water, a closed harbor, warming,
words opened up, forced the hinge of shell,
the fragile genie—my blue-eyed Muse—
El Patio where the world goes dizzy.

I sing in Spanish, too awkward
to move to El Cielo's lead. Un Rosaria,
a chain of silver commands. I am a country girl.
Numbers escape me 'till the morning I open
my cradle and display my array: the snowy mist
of intimacy and an ache on the tongue.
My heart waits on a horizon, blown and early,
a corner of too many leaves and arrivals:
*cama, flor, calór.* Lo que hace back when
the force beats back, a mile an hour look
looks back: a vocabulary of dust and
blade. Some things don't translate, what
this kid could never say.

## Not A Poem for Francísco X. Alarcón
## Who Wanted A Love Poem Before He Died


How can I write you a poem?
Every word flattens into sand-dollars,
Crumbles with the decay of memory;

How can I write you a poem?
Words are Old Pesos worth less than
Their silver. Your silver! How handsome!

You have become! Brother Water Moon
To my Sun On Earth, mi familia, twin-
Driven by Muse, Herself (twin to that, too),

My confidante, who knew then
How handsome you would become?
Your brilliance shows on your face,

At last. How can I write you a poem?
I want your certain flame to stay. I want
Your "Good evening!" again. I want your fire.

How can I stop this burning multiplicity?
I will you to the River of Light with these words—
Impudent masses, total recall. I want you here.

Heal! You're not ready for sainthood yet,
Carnal (as much as I know how much
That would please you). I pray with your poems.

I image in the blazing ball of Yo
Alone in his single cell of execution,
The cross one has to bear—and love.

Love clusters to your core, the ore
Of ages in your blesséd jaguar's eyes (same
Blesser of my father's final journey) (same ailment).

(I cannot let you pass.)
(I can/not believe.) Be live
Wire in your stalled jeep some lonely road,

Your single word on the radio—or
Whatever comes to pass. We, youngest kids
On the poetry block, now old fogies/Elders.

Let the decades come in triplets, my
Old friend. Once it was, you were the only one
Who even knew where I lived, or if....

This, too, shall come to pass.
Our Spirits, braided; our feathered path
Bound in poetry's laser wire, our Spirit-To-All

Deliverance: the largest life of all
Is yet to live. You have yet to live
To write the poem that saves us all.

# Instruction Manual for the End of The World

There's wood on the trucks.
The empty wait to fill.
This is the way you deplete
the forest, level the land,
skim and scum for profit.
This is the way you skimp
and scam: the man on the button,
the label on the bottle
made of paper made of wood,
made of would and could.
One by one thousand they go,
Living monuments, nesting trees,
the killing trees go, finally free
of their nooses. Nestlings, ground
to plywood, mashed to pulp.
The demolishers do their duty,
round up the usual suspects,
the tropical and nearly extinct,
the rare and agéd angels
of the future, past
and present danger.

Save lives. This is how
you save the world.

## The Trees' First Thought Is a Hilltop Without Trees

That old barrio bush, the baobab
tree that grew through the cracks
and spittle. I never knew the name
of her. Half palm, half fan, half elm,
too many halves to be something
more than nada. El arbol del
olvidó. It grew in every construction
zone, every disturbed mind, an unnamed
thing longing for Puerto Rico, a displaced
song aching for a finger to play, a paddle
to row, to sail El Caribe, that giant country.
I give this pledge of allegiance
to the named ones: those spangled
maples, the weeping willow, the dinosaur's
ginkgo. It's a pushy ass, that green brass
from a seed that will not die, the inner
growth that will not top.

# Love Song for the Burning

I still flip my tortillas
with my fingers. Same as with my men.
My gra'ma tried to teach me
not to. Always playing chicken
dinner on a plate, the way
to go, an empty gate. I linger
over flare. The mesmerized clear
the decks. A singe begins the trace.

In the morning the bullets lie
to know one. Many cry. The difference
between the rich and us is that death
for them makes families richer while every coffin
is a vote for poverty's wages. The sages
tell in history, La Maya, La Chichimeca...
Toltecan ruins rebuilt. The sacred
stones scavenged for Christian churches.

The expelled expel, Los espulsados
fill the pews. One genuflection too many
upon the riven land. The rivers swell
with bloat. The missing girls. The children.
The children with their cut out hearts
on their sleeves, a number on their wrists
written in the Sharpies they sell the military
made from extracted riches in a foreign land.

## To Wander and Be Weary

is to slave, slave the way a slab
of slate works for the heart,
the way a wave works for the shore,
the way trees slave for the air
or before the axe, slave the way
the track holds for the train.

I am away from work, but weary
of love. I am away from freedom
and weary of the bell. I am away
from the calloused palm, the bleeding
thumb, the eyes rubbed raw with peach
fuzz before the boiling vats and acrid
steam. I am a worker with the face
of a slave.

My grandmother held to her dance
and vanished the invisible chains.
My grandmother, sold from family at 12,
her weary knuckles, her flawless heart,
getting it all, clean; some other's filth.

## Brass Band

*for Alphonse Lewis*

Thank you to my homeroom teacher
for leaving me for hours under a tuba.
Too heavy to lift, it caged me in my band
chair for making something more than music.

Thank you for your musical hands, my color,
for your stories of women too pure
to touch your "filth," for helping her up
to her seat anyway: you, the composer,

a Beethoven, but Black. Thank you
for getting stuck in that barrio junior high,
for making the best of us, for fighting
for our right to die and be buried with

the rest, for teaching me to question,
for making me keep my head down
in order to imagine; for telling me to never
mind my ragged rolled skirts, the broken

toed shoes from Jesus Saves bins on Thursdays.
Thank you for leaving me there to own
my perpetual late, my too far ahead, my
never going to get there, my failure now

remembering your name. You are
forever etched in brass.

## TO DAVID: A Late Early Century Love Poem
## On Valentine's Day from T.K. On Presidents Day, 2017

*for Tk & David Landazwi* from *Love Poems To Strangers*

Who is more exotic than whom?
You, with your unrhymeable you?
Me with this reverse invisibility, my Super
Power. Power up with past power over
To power to, to that final destination:
That brave new heart: the dark.
The power with. How you lack
The taste of the green and healing
Bitter herb, so sweet to me; but not you,
My missing gene, for smell. We divide
The pizza. One eats up the leftover
Cilantro and sacrifices the Sacred
Rose, for you, my rare true color
Blind male. You, omnivore, to you
The rest is "mud."
                    How did you
Step out from the pages of my history?
My Basque descendant, my lifelong
Fascination, now as then, world without
End. Something in the clay. One, of old
Oil and limestone grit. One, true blue black
With the finest ring, with the invincible
Smile, multihued plates like armor on
An American armadillo.
                        I love you
Into dusk if it's day and as the loyal
Moon, you, glow until dawn where I'll
Discover you again. Here where
It's safe, where our love is a basket:
Both woven and grown—your greatest
Gift to me—your impossibly colored
Eyes: laziness, your greatest fault.

My lion king, no lyin', luxuriously lazing,
Lounging. You deserve me. I deepen
You. Together and apart, peat and moss,
Deep pool and ice. We floe, Slomo,
The Greatest Time On Wheels: our
                        Maltese Fulcrum

So big it takes eight spark plugs just to take it down
The street, each spark, the size of a fully known
Human being. Your love is this big. I knew first
Time we were on it. Lazy heart (as is this One.)
Lazy one that will stay where I lay. Let's keep on
LaLaLaughing, Love. O! Our LandofWhee!
My unpronounceable name! How we slay!

It's any age for you!
Glacier or the one we make.

Always out of step. A cradle (not the yoke)
Of love, together, in love. We trust

Just love.

## Pulling the Ivy: A Novena/
## A Love Poem to Donald Trump

*for Bob*

I

My last lover's body did shine
moonlit and chicken-skinned, his pelt
between Lutheran legs, soft, red
and white between blue blooded
rivers and sinews and sorry nicks. My
last lover's body aged past perfection.

Part 'Squatch, part Denisovan,
my last lover's great body extended
across the immigrant continents—
not even a Pilgrim on my stolen soil.

I will not say, he looked like you. Part
beast and no beauty save for peculiar.

My last lover's body bathed, and bade.


II

The last time I died I bathed and bade
my Spirit goodbye. The last time
a part of me died the vision lingered
on: a spent girl in the fogged up mud, splinters
of abandoned buildings wedged in her sole.
The Jesus Saves shoes, all foil and holey,

sloughed off… sure as my skin still left
in its sticky husk. How did I discover
the entire new world of my hearty survival?
We who push back the bear get reprieve

I guess. I left off believing when an entire continent
died inside me, slaughtered; its slender

Turtle Island left raped in the muck, some hard awakening.

## III

Storm troopers form bunkers, storm. Storm's hard awakening
banking my former home, still for the time it takes
to write it. To write saved her life, that
slave of the past, part beast, part burden,
a full woman with no past nor a name save
slave. These were the Peace Keepers, Beaders, Ones

Who Built The World's First Plank Boats. They bred us
for genius: all it took was "one drop of European
Blood." Blood lust. Blood lost. Blood on that morning
you left me on Kristallnacht... never to speak again.

A beast of burden, I bent my back to feed. Feel love
pouring from hands that knew you, hands that lock

your door against the ones, those real, who love me dead.


## IV

To The Ones Who Love Me Dead: How you feel
standing in front of a Pacific Ocean is different
from the Native who IS the WATER Herself.
This whole Earth I breathe breathes me. I am
The Land, a holy relic. There is no land between us
only the fear of sailing. Fear of the unknown. Fear Monster

Hunger. Hunger. Hunger. Herself. It was a cold continent
that drew you here like pus from the wound on my land.
The rape of nature that is your science (your Bacon
on the pan of Earth) your "birthright" my Destiny.

While Destiny walks a silenced street with Liberty
far behind. In a dark alley with a darker foe: me.

This is how I feel looking at a gasping ocean: Breathless.

# V

Try to pull it all at once—it will leave you breathless.
May the last breath I take be neither a reminder
of a situation my house has witnessed: she was nothing
in his eyes... an animal, or worse. "Who would care?" The
loops in the chain reel on, whipping. The marks are skin
to skewer. Horror films in one's own home: this is what

I say when I speak of race. Not the race to win, the stuck
lamehorse, the sure thing thoroughbred. This is genocide
not a football game. My heart is not a mascot, my name
you've given, a person with a heart, it's not what I'm called by.

The People call me home—in a single reel of haunting:
my mother burned alive, her sacrificial body violated. Her land,

a representation, ash... I was never going to survive.


# VI

From a poet's perspective, I was never going to survive.
Would she have defended me? Goddess Earth gave me
Grizzly big as your home (now trap). An urge to flee, flight
but stay put. It comes in; dream or not. It enters your home:
The Race Thing, war, "politics" gone stone cold personal.
You ignore the death reports, real body counts, the cabinet

picks, fluid value in the volcano's eruption
in protest across the Nation's oil fields, warming
mines, waste meltdowns, missile silos... gold hearts
like flecks of El Salvadorean silicon in the rainbow

surf. I want it back. All of it. I want the Earth to go
like a loose dog left off the chain like buffalo, like Eagle

taking over, green to gold to red white and blue.

## VII

It was so red white and blue the day I left you,
animal haggard, four days a nonhuman—not
a word touch or glance. Where was the lover's
chant? My long longing body now cold, gone
umber where embers were. Love loses the house,
trumps the chance of change. Communication

jammed like gunfire, like straight to the heart, cauterized.
I loved you. Loved every minute of you. Loved
the alien animal you as you did not love the animal
you discovered you lived with. It's a hair trigger from pet

to prey. How did I spring that trap? What snare got me here
from there? The trains of Tenino haul proppant to secure

the fracture. Life opens into what it's like being an animal.


## VIII

This is what it's like to be an animal, man
don't skin me. I was around gutting King crab for love
while you were eating beings in caves. Here's what
the cold can bring: you stay inside so long your heart
is a shriveled raisin a farmworker died for. I won't die
for you—nor because of you. You can't kill me.

Underground I grow with the corpses. We can take
down all your billions. Hallow heart, hollow mind; less
the hollow words. We will write you to infinity. One plus
one equals a nation. Love plus one makes a family. We weren't

bred to go down. We aren't bread to feed your slaves. The Zombie
Apocalypse is before us, and we, my savvy sisters,

we're fully alive! We eat up dead men for immunity.

# IX

I'm pulling the ivy for immunity. The hard taste of dead men
filling the lines of what could be poetry. I go there again
and hold on. I don't give up. I was bred for survival.
My rhizomatous roots refuse to sever, resist
the cuts upon us: the rubber bullets, the flash grenades,
the scramble brains and water cannons. Truth doesn't root

out. It is the Earth. You may think a golden glow
sets you apart but The Earth will dream you drowned.
Spirit in the form of returned buffalo come down to the fences,
under the wire. No wall can keep what has always been here out.

For millennia I loved this land I'm due. I love still, without it,
no matter what you do to me, have done, will do

to my children's family: I will root it out—and love.

*Thanksgiving, 2016*

## *April In Olympia*

*(a cruel month of daily poems with given titles)*

*"April is the cruelest month…"*
Again.

# With Crooked Teeth and Bones

*for Alisa Valdes (Rodríguez)*

The first word is illegible
so ineligible for what I am about
to do. A woman may commit suicide today,
an April Fool.

An April Fool "with crooked teeth
and bones" comes out next, clearly defined.
(He said he liked me best for my "wanky" teeth
like his.)

Like his suicide… this one, smarts
and shines, a Luminous Lady with her life
on hold, only known (only love)
through a lit cellphone.

Through a lit cellphone she waits until notice.
I return to first words, that tear-stained slip, that
scribbled halo of hand in manner or manor
I can't decipher.

Who are we to decipher? We walk the narrow lane
home without a friend. "Choosy" it reads? Too chunky
for "Classy" as I turn it over and see from the other side,
"Chones" (as in dirty ones.)

"Chones!" You Dirty Girl! Exiled to the NYC turmoil
and brew. Bruja you, still you spelled, you swelled
swell in the word and secure in your world,
your brilliance and beauty.

Your brilliance and beauty will be remembered last
unlike (we) of the crooked teeth and unset bones
(disfigured walker, dreams on stunted stilts).
You made your way.

You made your way, a Dirty Girl, but sayin.'
You of the love sonnet, you of the secret
villanelles: how well we thought
we knew you.

We know you now, know trauma to trauma,
a mispronunciation if any footnote at all
added as an afterthought (a better lot
than ridicule).

How can they (then) ridicule you? That's not what
this is about. It's about turning the page, the clarity
rediscovered there: the word that saves
(on the page).

Keep it on the page and hold—don't fear the dance
alone. Taste through malnourishment from the moistest places.
Female of the traumatized race, survive! (I do. We must!)
Our first word is "Choices."

*4/1/15*

## Bell Peppers

The hottest piece is seed. We, three
bad girls under a moon: La Niña, La Pinta
y una Santa María moonlighting to a trio
of gusts: the brawny, the rusty, the blade.

Far off a hillside was cawing
over the canopy of highrises, banks
of turtles fought for survival by the still
creeks, the rills of this tiny nation.

All we saw was us and no one
saw us. We clustered on the rooftops,
ladybugs flown home and back. Back
to the roots and brambles, back to that

fine infinitive. We swelled our moons
and past, the wee feet beneath us, finally.
Hot as want or nipped in the bud
we flavored everything, expressed and rung.


*4/2/15*

## Break the Glass

Break the glass! Feel!
The rest is just that: rest
of the story. Story it up.
Stay with it. Tend
it. Husband it. Be a being
that frees. Don't hold it.
Let it go so it never comes
back. Break the glass. Refuse
to be a bit part in that movie.
The eye trains the sky; the sky,
the clouds. All we see is we.
All I need is we; me, too.

*4/3/15*

## Blood Moon, II

Last night I watched you
disappear, all shadow, sliver,
shard, a stepping into dimness,
dark and storm, your glow, redelivered.

I read it through the yews, a magic
flickering, the golden ring, now on/
now off, an idle promising, a long division
from what is cloud drift, what is slide.

I saw you, crisp, a not-imagining, then
left you, a vanishing, more there than light
for fact of a past, and passing. I choose
not to miss this leaving, this deliverance.

4/4/15

## Burden

*"I'm gonna lay down*
*My sword and shield..."*


*Down by the riverside....*
The Sound opens from its teary
banks to fresh waves of sweet
spring fillings. Glorious birds
whet the way to whack. *Hay caballo/*
*vamos por el monte.* Raven gathers,
old crows remind. Strength, more than
a word to steel. Old growth timber
line the passageways as those who have
sell and clearcut. Here, I am,
never home but here, an import,
an anti-commodity. What looks
like fire is really rain—not on the plain
but a halo of hail upon the mountainside—
a kind of healing, a resurrection.

Friends write of love and war,
the nevermore never far from the lips,
send dollars and sense as I presume
to live here. Here, where no soil loams
but the many baskets of needles to gather,
clear, compost. Not even a worm wants
to stay. There's no digging down
for the roots. Down by the riverside I lay
my burden down. Another wants
to kill herself. I come up, salmon,
dancing my way to mercy. Joybound,
I stubbornly open, toned by the wee
birds calling; seeds long past their date
refuse to expire. Another season
of spring and load—another year
not yearning.


4/5/15

# Family

You said we were family
then disappeared over the arch
of the heart. Marsh grass knows
the way. The wind blows north,
south bends. Marmots reveal
themselves along the highways of my
past. Old growth burns. Pine
survives, sprouts. Volcanos blow
after millennia. I salvage the stones,
savage here in my radiance, dust
off pebbles of deep grey, the hieroglyphs
scribbled there, an age. Blessed
in this decade—it is sometimes enough:
the blue sage, the silence. Living
on the earth is never easy—for some
choose the stars. There is another
ray through forest grey, the burning
off of fog, the passing through,
a moving on.

*4/6/15*

## "Did You Hear What They Said?"

*after Gil Scott Heron,*
*for Nestora Salgado & for those who fast*

They said another mother's dead,
dead and can't be buried. 43 children
disappeared after capture. Another mother
cries for half a millennium in the desert
searching for her daughter's daughter
(the deserts of our country, the only crop
remaining.) Hear what the mothers are saying.
They are Constitution bound. They are found
as the many remains in a waste, an arroyo.
Fill the heart with what another mother
is saying. Rise up in unison, a voice
for the chorus of peace. Another wave
is added to the saving waters. Here,
in Anahuac, The Place Between Two Great
Waters, all of the unburied join in. Feast,
sing between the weeping. Did you hear
what they are saying? Women and children first.

4/7/15

## Hidden Love

I won't be your hidden love,
your underground grove, your grotto,
your whole lotto in a drawer. I won't be
in your b-grade movie, a tela in a box.
I won't be your native daughter, not
your leaping final salmon. I won't be
forgotten. I'll be tied to the thread
of your tale. I'll be tailed and shadowed,
a dime feature, a bed of dreams. I'll be
shreds of a momento, a slugfest
in the stew of you, a sudden squall
and an aftermath. I am the stone's throw,
the target and the sling. I won't be your anything
but this, your hidden love, my bliss.

*4/8/15*

## In The Engine of My Throat

In the engine of my throat
beats the heart, that stubborn
all in all, that so and so.

*4/9/15*

## Fililatinos

The ocean is an immense country
unbound by land, the sea seizes
us and claims us in her wake.
Land doesn't define us, only the jungles,
soft paws under the canopy, trees,
our bloodline. The ocean is a giant
nation. Mother magnet to the Four
Directions, the people come. Some sail,
some stay. The People, forged by flood
and famine, gente del mar, know the waterways
of this Nation. Keeper of the Calendario,
knowledge of tides and stars, perpetual
time in this nation of ocean, nuestra cultura.
Father Typhoon, Mother Huracán, mistress of the seas,
you hail and we obey. Forgotten songs,
the forgotten Orishas still beat in the hearts
of those unforgotten: We, The People of the Sun
and sea, del delfín y jaguar, of tapir
and mono. Bobo calls through the leaves
and the bulldozing. Something in the veins
remembers, distilling us down to
what we were, together, members of
a huge country: El Mar, Gente of work
and the long wait—and wake.

*4/10/15*

## Sandhill Cranes

*after Jane Goodall*

100,000 cranes return
so why can't you?

Clouds of loving
before the nest

Mounds on mounds
the still and the moving brown

Blossoms of wings
the lumbar steady

Every craning neck
hosts a crest of black and white

The final decision
never is until the flight

Dancing under moonlight
the lit leaves shudder

Around and around they go
lakeside, hillside

By your side
beside myself with eclipse

Shadow blooms
into 100,000 cranes

Returning.

*4/11/15*

## Reconciliation

*for Afred*


How can I bury you, my one
True (dead) Love? No thing is so
ultimate a truth. Everything else
is load and weigh; flesh, the whey;
no way, the chaff. I reconcile myself
with you, not even a dream: a letter
on the page, with you, the sudden spring
without you. (This is what it feels
to be aborted.) How can I ever feel
you again? Who will card me into felt?
Do I pass on my precocious pillow?
To have loved you fully with that youthful
feeling between old friends turned lovers;
or, to have never felt you, but felt you
as I appeared in your last sueños. Last
I loved, I thought of you; Discovered
you in a single silver thread of dead
hair on the living, and remembered how you
(*You*) loved me—and I loved—reconciled.


*4/12/15*

## Moldering Rocks Listen to Things

Moldering rocks listen to things
with memories longer than the most ancient
trees. Read the hieroglyphs therein.
Before The People painted petroglyphs,
centuries of wind, millennia of millions
of leagues of rain etched upon that face.
Before The Great Destruction, before fire
forged a Nation, before you or the wee
worries there was rock. There was eruption
remaking, iron refertilizing. There was red earth
and secret snow. There was ice listening
to rivers floe, icebergs glistening. Hear the drought
creaking beneath your feet? Be stone in the
response ability. Water into Life—That's all
we own. The rain won't matter without us.

*4/13/15*

## Notes

Looking for notes I discover
this note that says, "NOTES."
Just like that and just like that
a poem fashions itself. Out of the bungalow
of loneliness it tends cuidado. Folded
for so long, it's easily overmissed.
It's passing for official but it's just a piece
of paper, however lined. Other notes
are evident as tags, slips or slip-offs,
that draw attention to themselves
as they might be a part of something important.
I find them in my shoe. They fall over themselves
when paying for meat. They crowd the caverns
of my bag (never a purse) and fill my moves.
It's so expectant of the pickup
and notice, all there like a girl
with her love letters longing for a lost boy
with empty pockets to come and stash her.
So easy to throw away, to dump. Telling.

4/14/15

# Constipation

He was a hero in his own country,
a falling star who could do no good.
He was zero on a chart of river, the ever
spring of summer. He was everything. He was not
an organization, not the president of his heart.
He was an art of lovecraft, a way out
of trouble. He was his own good. He was bad
for nothing. He was the lost stitch in a blanket
of souls. He was anything but sorry, any tale
at all was at his beck and call. He wasn't
ever listening. He was his own record holders.
He was 86 on a scale of 69. He was better
when no one was looking. He was a good looker,
a dead soul on arrival. He was long coming.
He was alone in his garden. He was a nation
of fools. He was what we all were waiting for,
he was a lone chair in the forest. He was a bicycle
held by moss. He was green as you can get.
He was ungettable. He was still making them wait,
a constipation of character, a ration of waste.


*4/15/15*

## Much Abides

Too much abides. Not enough settles.
I stretch the film of my days and nothing
sticks. I'm going farther again, a once
or seldom travel. I'm going far in
my head in order to miss you. I'm missing
nothing instead. No thing passes me
or if it does it tides me to no notice.
I'm living long from my future. I'm a past
participle of time. I am longing here
indefinitely. I'm a gentle swell, swell
and leaving. I'm an epic tide beginning. I'm
the wave to end all your ondas. One dunk in me
and it's sure to sail you. Love, it was just
a beginning. Why make it an end? Much abides
in a reinvigorating kiss, a miss, a chance
dance in love with a new and me, abiding.

*4/16/15*

## A Flag

It was just a flag after all,
a subtle reminder of the fly
on your flyaway wall. You put up
a stall and our lava waved it away. I wanted
to be a breeze, a play of ways. I wanted us
to be. But it was just a piece of white
remembrance, bit of loose stitching, a scrap
of blue. Blue that I remember you, I'm pulling
up daisies, letting the squirrels plant my seed.
I'm feeling you away and it's as banks
to the sea, some endless shoring. It was
just a flag afterall, a red stall, some
kicking in my native hall, a longhouse
where no one recalls how to pray. I thought
you were my native language. I thought you
Desire, a pansy in my side, I crusted over
the soil pushing to blossom you. You, the rock
on my chest, my seedling. Somebody flew
you and you dragged to the ground with the lack
of wind. I was only a blow, a whistle when
wet. It was only a flag after all: a red one.

*4/17/15*

## Hands

These are the hands from which we speak,
the mouths that teach us the halves we are
when left apart. Apart, I can handle the rain,
each choice, each choosing the air to fall in;
into a puddle of you, I fell, hands over knees.

It was a long beginning, a shorter ending,
only five fingers long, a wet countdown.
My hand was up when I chose you, an easy
answer. I memorized you by heart so
the absence of you is a shadow I can trace.

Holding you to heart, I begin again, a long
slow process, a quick fix. Hand over hand
I surmount, and surrender. I put my hands in
your pocket for a treason in this country between us.
Handed down by you I will choose again, again,

hands down.


4/18/15

## Strawberry Shortcake

I'll call you, tailing you on the donkey.
Crumby dumpling, I'd salute you
but you're gone. Deep in the cream,
("Mexican women are such fresas!")
I wonder at the past of you. Not even
a name to your ruddy face, an exclamation,
a travel. What Clyde are you that you desire
this Bonnie? What ride are you that you hide
this bone inside your trunk? Whipped by you
to a froth and bear, I amble back from which
I came. Coming to you, I parted some leaves,
left some, leaving a trail of slime behind, perhaps.
But it was sweet. Though the good stuff was only
air and the protein of us, incomplete. You & I, matter
and a simple syrup. Lap me again, lick
the stamp and send me. Strawberry Shortcake, my
once in a while, you have me going back to childhood,
a rememberer, believer in fidelity, in the recipe.
Tart and sour indefinitely, Sunday treat, I'm going
to make like a banana, and split.


*4/19/15*

## Temperance

*"To marry him is hopeless,*
*to be his whore, witless."*
*— Shakespeare "The Two Noble Kinsmen, II, IV, 4-5*

Temperance is a virtue
along with chance and fortitude.
There is no patience
for the willow refusing the wind,
there is no gratitude too deep
nor word too shallow.

I hold this to the fire:
soft metal me that gleams
and gleans, hard diamond
that resists the cluster,
my resistance to the blaze,
(your face, the color of ash.)

After you are spent
remember the copper
that forged you, relive
the tight squeeze, the tightening
warmth. Some things will carry
you, some will hold you together.

After I am gone:
hummingbird, bumblebee,
wolf flowers (their gaping mouths,
a place for thirst, for beaks).
Every day I test the blade,
"Cleave or stay... Cleave or stay..."

and stay away.

4/20/15

## Burning Limbs Falling as Amulets Across the Sky

It was burning limbs falling as amulets
across the sky. It was a full-scale attack.
It was ash and heat and fallout. It was
safe and at a distance. In the distance the flare up
crosshatching its way across our separate lives.
The long road between us, already a thing of the past.

I watched it burn in my dream, my native home.
Home was a trick math quiz, a burning desire
to score. You bore into me. The black expression,
a smile in disguise. How much of you I stored,
piled you into magical pyramids of decisions
I can't take back. I can't take back the spring.

It was a long winter lit by the flint of our
striking. It was a togetherness of moss, the substance
of a rainbow no one sees. Across the skies of your arrow
flaring, an amulet from Cupid's broken necklace.
I touched you and I was touching stone. The decay,
evident; the longing, lasting; spark dust, burning limbs

and all.


4/21/15

## Black Rock

You gave me a black rock, kept
the one in the shape of a heart: a fractured
masterpiece, another's millennium's waste.
I wander once your lanky path, and pause.
Light cat paws in the dew, the new of you
fresh and on my mind, a constellation of stars
I have no map nor memory to traverse—my travois
long and in disuse. Once there was a horse
and I could cut through the weeds. Fir needles
not enough to inoculate against the sudden cold.
In frigid air it rests in my hands, a touchstone
lacking the master's touch. I ground this rock
slowly, and take an age to think you out. How everything
can change. The strings of time are held up by whim.
I win you over, lose and spin again, swirling
my metals in search of the glint. I give you.
words you'll never read, and sieve the silence.


4/22/15

## From Inside the Breath Comes a Feather

From inside the breath comes a feather,
torrent of wings, longing to belong.
This flock inside flaps its hunger.
A hundred thousand cranes, a rare hummingbird,
something long extinct, like love, roves.
I hold the final word taut to the chest.
I hold it in and breathe. A thousand promises
of pillows, a single cover of warmth. I hold this
air in—a 100,000 barbs you will never feel.
I hold this flapping, this dumb lung: the heart.
I hold it aloft, touching the trees with the ghost
of it. I hold it inside, a feather when the goose
has gone. The fox steals away the night. A love
takes flight. All the earth agrees in Spirit. It's
this path or that, low on the ground or Light.

*4/23/15*

## Anticipate

I don't anticipate the ending. I do not
mourn the past promises lain to waste. Land
I love, you were a gray cloud passing, and I,
the sun. What is expectation to the heart?
Its dumb luck is to beat or not. A mindless pacing,
a monotonous dance you still must watch, is this
the grand entrance at work? I sift the clods,
chuck the cones, let the sharpest refuse lie. All
you were was metaphor. Seeds never flared into
renewed life. I pare the fruit down to a single
portion. This one's for you, for your ardor of moment.
I let you lie. Unheard, I nevertheless searched
for songbirds in the mossy boughs. I expected
age to temper me. I had never met your match.
I anticipate another living, another loving on its own.
The long walk lit by a patchwork of sun may
not grow the crop. It's a circular path, a patch
of dirt owned by another. I live this mulch,
don't anticipate a start, and hunker down to new.


4/24/15

## Living Ectoplasm

*for The Procession of the Species*

Last night I was a luminous being
marching for the extinct like me, once
deemed a terminated "race." We danced, humans,
joyous for life itself. Lit from within,
our exotic talking protoplasm swayed to ancient
drumbeats. We forgot our divisions, embracing
the fragile. All of existence stood still so
that all would exist. The living procession
under paper and sticks, waving itself back
into tribe. I felt alive. Under stars and starfish
and the Great Blue Heron like the one I friended
who was my size, who sat beside me, mourning,
on the bank, close enough for an arm around.
Four eyes gazing into a mucky river at salmon still
determined to spawn. Still we breed. We love and
grow. I, the almost extinct of our species, lay down
my arms. The sheep and cattle replaced by White
Rhinos and pandas. I bear the loss in this rebirth,
this living global consciousness, and weep
for us all. I wept for joy, for us—for All!

*4/25/15*

## Ash

It all comes down to this: ash
in the kitchen; ash, the bed; ash in my
graying head. I had had enough of ash.
There wasn't enough vinegar in the world
to clean it. I scrubbed at that legacy, my fairytale
poverty, the shoes that fell apart, the toe
in the dike of my future, barely holding. Now I turn
the earth, nurture worms in my refusal to just
die. I shovel ash, wait for bloom. Once I lived ash,
wondered which of the flakes were hers. His anger
(something) did this, I would murmur to know one. Alone
we give up; alone, we reduce to ash. His action, now
a part of every burning. The reels go by, the news
thickens with plot. I stand alone under the sapling fir
and water, feed. I am not alone here, under the trees
in this immense forest of willow that we are: bending.
Bending, I am led to you, a river, sound, a slow music
of clouds banking the way. I follow her, the spring,
and know what to do with this burning (lack). I remember
autumn, something like forest, and do. I refuse to be
the board before the flame, the tree before the final fire.


4/26/15

## The Sun's Rays Burn Love Today

Come be animal and marsh.
Come be swimmer and dance
in flight. Come be all with all.
Come know it all. The Sun's rays burn
love today—though the ice caps
are melting, though true love is stranded
on an iceberg somewhere in the icy soup.
Come and free us from ourselves.
Come and save us. Save yourselves
in seed. The love cometh and the love
taketh away. Time to mourn is alone.
Together we do. Come and do. Come
and feel the morning dew on your feet
and walk in peace. Each one to a separate
journey. Come and travel thus: prepared
to heal the wounded, wind the springs
of Spirit, salvage the water, give love
and thanks to water. Let water absolve
our sorrows and thank it. Let us survive
the hurricane we've become to each other.
The Earth is in pain. The Earth is waking.
Know this: death every day.

4/27/15

## Blood

There was blood evidence and still
the culprit got away. There was surveillance
footage, a positive ID. There was a smoking
revolver. We know who did it. There was blood
on his shoes. There were fingerprints
on the trigger. There were eyewitnesses.
There were multiple videos. There was power
of the press. Attorneys are involved. It was
a done deal, an open and shut case. It
was justice or bust. The blood was on
the wall, a message is written in the empty
street. There were no sidewalks. There
was no way to abide. It was an abomination,
an outrage. The people are outraged. This is
not the way lives are supposed to be. This is
a free world, a free country, a free one walking,
a free America. Free America. Free all
who walk therein. No man is created
unequal. We are all women on the face
of The Earth. We walk in beauty in the shadow
of the police. All hail the barrage of gunfire
upon us. All notice and hail, the hail of blood
this time.


*4/28/15*

## Death Breath

On the final day the final
day had become. How you are never
prepared. When it happens to you
(and it will) will you be shifting
the drive around the stages of grief?
Have you heard the death breath
of the planet yet? We hear the rumblings
of earthquake and fire. An ancient
prophecy awaits. The Great Turtle awakens.
We live in its shadow; we, who are shadowed
by crows. Our death lives here, a secret
inside. We come outside to save
our souls. We revolt in the living.
We do away with death inside. All outside
is heard though few listen. For those
for whom the last gurgle tolls, we,
family together: grief, our home. All
life is legend. The rest is work. Let us
work together in what we love. Let us love
unto our last death breath. Let's do it together.
Live!

*4/29/15*

## Studies Have Shown

Studies have shown an axis is shifting.
All of time is a changing of the planetary
guard. Come and heed this. Studies have
shown that love cures all: the magma,
the thinning, the destiny, the lying, all
of construction in a no-life zone. Studies
have shown there's been enough studying.
Time to love. Time to free the data. Time
to be-leave. Time to tree. Dreams have
revealed what it is to wake up. Death has shown
too much killing. What is at stake is what
goes through the heart, what silver lining lines
inside. Stop lying, studies have shown,
and love truths out. Let the truth out. Be
a thousand pages reading. Be the book you
will to be. Be here now, picking up. Studies
have shown, those who pick themselves up finish
with the rest. Be the rest. Don't give up. Rest
is all you need. The sad singers say it best:
"Love is all you need." Last word in any poem is
Love.


*4/30/15*

*Destination Anywhere*

# Destination Anywhere

*after Allen Ginsberg*

I have watched the best Souls of my Nation
Crumpled in foil against the crumbling brick
Barefaced of ivy. Yanked out, cranked out
Yodeling their terror through the copped streets battered
Blind of ambition and terrorless: one Nation divided
Under God in the misunderstanding states of America
(Some far away seasalt, past flaring), a tattered flag's last
Gleaming. *"Blood on the street. Blood on the street!*
*Look at the blood on the street!"* They shout at the boarded
Up ministries of destiny while Destiny, a girl with no face
Is Pregnant with horror: "The faces! The faces!"
Have you ever seen such drunken blue on your blue
TV screens? Nothing is ever yellow but the dead to the poor.
The Poor lose wits, The ocean grows vast with their fears.
They have no more hands in which to relieve their thirst
Of themselves. No more feet with which to run. They are
Light. They levitate, snagged on the thought of themselves
At last! The start to the blackening aid. Follow them!
The ones still rowing ashore chained to the metal
Are gold. The streets full of gold! The death markets
Are busy! All the engines, their minds at full
Throttle. While someone is locked in there, erased and foreign.


Oh! I know you don't know this.
They moan in the night. Their shopping carts
Rattle tattle to the busy hum of the burning
Computers inside the core dream of Freedom!
Ringing in their shot-out ears! On Freedom! On past
The debilitating. On past the commodity cheese
Fed generations of waste, the telemarketers of addiction,
Faces, more Indian than not. The knot in the shadows
Calling to us under The Mystery Tree and their cattle.
Their tobaccoless longing and coffeestained
Faces demand, more longing fear in blue.
"The trees! The trees!" Why must we level! Why
Must we murder the long summer, the vision of one?
The plan, the disaster, the revision of the summit, over.
All we are is All. All we can is a long division of over.

The call and response is overdue, overpaid to some else.
Same destination, some crossroads, some X on
The map to the Heart of the Matter. What is the matter
With You? Catgut of your sawed-off tongue? Don't
You know who you are? The pawl-bearers. The Kaddish
Speakers, quorum of won, the you you speak, fleshless
And pure. We know what we speak. The dead know well.
We speak to your quarry of one, to the fish in your belly
Drinking your spittle: the devein divine unto the night
Into King Dom Cum, some lost longing, sour trudging,
The war done, some lost languages trailing behind with
Their bleeding teats—trudging nigh on the white horse
In a chant and fire; some long into it, some show, some slow
Download to what's due you had the speed and soft
Ware been true. There is a place that maters. (sic)
Between the arms, the bruised hip and less the lip. Some full
Mouthed filing, some shutting up but not to say
There will never be enough words of love for their tattered
Remains, what remains. They stay in vermillion sunset but don't know
That word or its meaning, flashing the maw. They loss for no one
For no one knows them. They talk to shoes searching for pennies,
Some slot to pick, some farthing to travel to but it's a long good buy
And it's the wrong day to go and the banks are closed to crowd
At River's Way, to those who walk. The shadows on the Goddamned
Golden Bridge know the Goddamned Way: facing home
On a long dare. Love gone long! Always laughing, their speech
Lacking syllables. They speak gibberish but it's okay. No one's listening.
Always longing, their hearts in beer-cupped hands, the ones they still
Have stuffed deep in their empty. They speak for themselves.
They have a long row to hoe counting on North for fishes,
Broken grammar, the loaving of their constant labor, their arduous
Loving. They are all about themselves, stumbling. The day is a dare
In the mauls of the dogs who look in smudged windows at the shows of
Tomorrow but do not see them or speak our language, dry as it is
With gravel. They are mute. Their slack jaws are full of stuck
Eggs. They get away with it, too. The ones we don't shoot get
Beaten. They kick away and just get beaten until they are shot
Up with IT. *"The horror! The horror!"* The horror we speak.
But it has no referent to the year less
                              Earless.


I have known the far off best minds, the lines of spittle
Oozing down their noses like from the mummified

Cannery janitor who works all night for a dime allergic to peaches,
Whose hands are red though their skins are black.
They write poetry to each other in the muted dark, there in
Their curtainless windows revealing their hide. They speak
To no one, frantically pumping Ganesh's tusk into their loin.
There they are certain. They duckwalk zigzag in their flopping
Soles, their mouths pursed in a circular "Oh?" The silos of mysteries
Sealed from their kiss, their Souls are dingy damage in the light.
*"The Light! The Light!"* I have seen The Light! I have seen them.
They speak but it wasn't at us. Not we. Not the indivisible.
They walk the waking streets reeking of popcorn and white
Chocolate. The poop on the street, ubiquitous and chalky.
They scattershot easily. Their minds have been elsewhere.
It is all they know of flushing, now flashing. The backup slapping.
The little brown girl begging for coin again, to sell the painted
Rock, its perfect rose chipped off in the fall: that girl is me.
She never recovered waiting for a man to take her away
To some pay-and-save of the heart's delight, some valley
Of craw. *Lo,* that I might see you, they pray to each other
In the red alleys of the demeaning sheets. They live where
They can. She never recovered from that man, the velvet
Trauma. Frightened by a child in the street, her good red
Coat flapping in the rein like the winds of butterfly, the anger
Of nice on her face. She wasn't afraid of me. She feared.
Her love who led her away, nameless and vivid. *Why?*
Why did she never reason with me? A direct child?
An urchin, a Dickens of a Dickens, a Dickensonian
Edge to it all and everything. Everything settles. A woman
Alone is unnerving. She is unnerved, that woman,
Stripped like a shrimp from what passes for time.
She is still afraid, marred forever by my much; never to
Repair the rose and the sorrow.
$\qquad\qquad\qquad$ At the dock, the dim
Lit reeking. My beauty sat in gum-stuck theaters rocking
Around the clock. The mice are asleep heavy with cat.
She should have kept her legs to herself, that kicking.
While I, babysat self, my money in hand, my baby
Belly asking who got in first? Who didn't lock the door?
Who faltered? What not did she put in her face? Some
Kind of marrow, an arrow of a girl, asking, again and
Gain. Why? Why do they always want to put it in
There? There, there. The man should have said
When he brought her to nowhere. Some special delivery.
He has given up on ever seeing her again as he takes

Her arm he doesn't want to touch and she breaths in
Panic of horses in a field of fire: at me, a small desire.
Is it there? I want to ask her, the low form, asking. I
Want to ask her, did it hurt like broken Binaca bottles
Going under the skin? Like shattered glass in the butt?
But like that, like fire? Sure, man, like that, like liar, like
Some tree. "Some man will make you pee your pants
If you don't lock the door." My grandmother warned.
It was like peeing your pants. I dreamt it smelt like flame,
Like Holy Water. The bruise still misting my vision,
But safe, some kind of arresting. Make me, Hermanita,
Make fire. They called in the bright. And I went for it.
Barefoot and mattered. My grandmother, terminated
At the edge of her deliverance, at the Maul at the end
Of 1842, of 1492 ways to gather your pennies and
Dream of good weather of every number that's ever
Been fought for; that's how to get ahead, fight for your
Numbers. Lock the door, I would have told her. She
Didn't. She didn't listen to her grandmother's wisdom
And now she has broken herself, this woman, the one
Who doesn't cave at the heart getting marked under
The great tires of Acme America or the man who takes
Her along for it, all fury at the one he would shoot
If he had a gun: a small me. The dead grow tired
Of guns. They whine for ice cream, some utterance,
Some fantastic joke like there used to be. They get
No respect. They are not on our cells unless we
Put them there, under your famous caul. I find
Some scribbled up. The X of the unalphabetized
Left unmarked for use or the six figure contracts
Of their multiple burials. They are one shoved,
Short of room you are going to go home to; the dirges
You sing, wake from; the wakes from the boats
Without cargo on the River Styx, the sticks, the old
Tules that skin them, flay away the only souls
They'll never know.


I have run down the lunatic streets holding
My painted satin skirt between my stiffening
Legs, together; I, wearing rags and feathers
From Salvation Army counters. I am holding
Together to the heart of me, and when The River
Sees me, it knows drowning men can't touch me.
And, when will the heavens open? Only nameless

Lives can hear me. They open their puny pockets
To the fog-struck morning, only the foreign sun
Thins this eve-struck land, this parched settlement
Where we wait, this Garden of the The Heart's
Delight and the memory therein. The seeds
Crush under the heavy trucks, blown away
By their wingless destiny (a woman running,
All the wild fear of her as she's blown away
By the tattered rattle of automatic gunfire
Unto matriarchy) filled the slots of men's asses
With coin while copulating masses heave under
Dry ocean's scratched sand and the hurricanes
Breathe for us and The Earth fumbles below,
Belly full of birth. I am in the night over and over
To get it out, each one. Each year, the wasting
Of my age. It is good to quantify. It calms
Down the doomy drunks with missing addition.
What is the good? They long for a second
Language and argue in the no reply. And The True
Stay gullible, waiting in their hearts for the raving
Seabirds, but all they get are the painted landscapes
To land. They are never getting, never tranced into puzzles
For their missing pieces. They keep it glued together
With eggs and stuck to the walls of their prisons. As
They are, it never works out, they crumble into pieces.
Their best calendars fade. The real estate agents
Retire into their comfortable mortgages while
The plastic spoons of the poor's tomorrow beg
For a fix, anything to fix it up tomorrow, la mañana
That never comes for the too raw rub. The woman
Will pay. (The man, lost to more photocopying
Of girls. Their slave screens holding the fingerprints of blue
If they were more than this dust under the cracks
And creaking floorboards.) They require the room
To die so they go outside where Freedom lives.
Their heads in their hands, their diploma from the
Crumbling peeking out from the bar like the small
Hand of the left-behind child left in the smoking car
While the weary sleep it off one more time. "One
Thing! One thing!" *Just one thing lacking...* They
Murmur to the jungle of one. The golfing judge,
The drinking healer begging their Fall. The churches
Ring on every corner of America iPlus; or would
Ring if they had a bell and believed in the bull.

The bell in the hall between hemispheres rings
But it's an arson fire and a melted telephone, old
School, and it rings off the hook while the hooks
And daggers of the young who serve wait for them
Gleaming in the night with their baskets of doom,
Their hollow man heels clicking a virtual echo
Behind them for one last time, one final thing.
"One thing!" One fling. One long golden bow,
The bough or the silvered screen where they
See who they really are, some half
Utterance, naked but fulfilling.

Till. Death do us Part.

One

Spirit-to-All.

*Summer Solstice, 2014*

*Sirens of Olympia*

## "Night Magic (Blue Jester)"

*After a painting by Carlos Almaraz
and poem by Féderíco Garcia-Lorca*


Blue that I love you
Blue that I hate you
Fat blue in the face
Disgraced blue that I erase
You lone blue
Blue of an alien race
Strong blue eternally graced
Blue that I know you
Blue that I chose you
Crust blue
Chunky blue
Moon blue glows that despise
You—idolize you
Blue and the band disappears
Blue of the single left dog
Blue of the eminent red fog
Blue that I glue you to me
You again and again blue
Blue blue of the helium
Bubble of loveloss
Blue of the whirlwind
The blue being again
Blue of the endless rain
Blue that I paint you
Blue that I knew you
Blue of the blinking lights
Blue of the landing at full tilt
Blue of the wilt
Flower of nightfall
Blue of the shadow
In yellowed windows
Blue of the blown
And broken glass
Blue of the Blue Line
Underlines in blue
Blue of the ascending nude
Blue before the blackness
Of new blue of our winsome

Bedlam Blue of the blue
Bed alone: blue of the one
Who looks on blue of what
Remains of cement fall
Blue of the vague crescent
Ship sailing blue of the rainbow
Of wait blue that I whore
You—blue that I adore you
Blue of the bluest door
Blue my painted city
In blue (it blew)

# In Another Woman's Garden

Shame or secret
Sacred pleasure
I re-home rocks

Launch wayward slugs
In my neighbors' direction
This ginger journey

Starts here
In the self
Where new lines

Fuse, where seedling
Love flares like moss
Hardy as lichen

I was a desert
Unto my Self
You, a divorced well

Something moist
But still rigid under
Big leaf maple

Refuse amid the duff
And danger of cap
And spoor

We remember nothing
Reimagined
In our hardening

Handled layers
We unemcumber ourselves
Lean into ripe sun

And grow
Our own seed
On salted earth.

## Grizzly Grace

I was dreaming
that moment when you're awake but realize someone
in your dream could be real—or something.
It was me I tried to save—and lost

or found
inside a silver suitcase like that lost
concha belt, Gra'ma's Native pride, the pounded
delicate butterflies, filigree feelers intact

or like that dripping August birthday
left alone with all my words lost in storage
or taken in subterfuge, in spite, for material
gain like a home that once had housed me.

Nevermore;
Myself—as object, a drawing of me, how
I found me: that half-wild girl, dog dealing
with a bear, a part of the ecology, surviving.

I was there
and knew exactly what to do. A matter
of when, and no more. "Lore..." folded in a book. A bird,
a turquoise tortoise fetish, Grizzly grace—escaping.

## Delphi

What is still? Frost
on a snowy day, the way
a cat looks lovingly,
a forest before the fall.
The small of the world hunker
in this lingering precipice in space;
Whole dimensions of loss on this continent
of me, we expand into who we really are
Today, of all days, certain passages
apply. The grand sequence of science,
suspended in the buzz of silence
Here the tree minds the earth.
I dwell here in heart's hearth
where the brave weary, far, where
the eclipse of summer twice feels
like an ice age breaking—and it is.

## Post-Solstice

(post-"Beetles")

I leave my trace in seed,
a stubborn root, bearing
the wait. Out of fashion
Flor de passion, cumbersome pumpkin,
something unpronounceable, forgettable;
forgotten fräuleins of California poppies
and feverfew punctuate the paragraphs
of pebbled beds.
    I sprout too tall
and gangly for the clime. English
Chamomile in a field of French
with not enough food on the plain
and not nearly sun. I light, too soon,
seed-wrecked on the rocky bank, alive
and livid with a secret ancient medicine.
There for the look; weed-like, but tasty.

## Making It

What makes the summer? Wild
rabbit, a gentle rain before the hard
frost, the wonder hand of spinach?

Gopher chooses where the garden goes.
Gummy worms go before gopher's last
meal. I feed fat maggot meal worms.

*To chickens! Wee! Go!* Without the pecking
order, things want to grow. Stone relents.
Scotch broom blooms over the lily field.

Willing circles from glaciers past, thick
clods of compost mushroom. Crow caws,
circling from the pack; mindful of the pact.

## Pact

A crow's uncertain possibility —
here, we have justice. Just us
under the green maple. I plow all
day by hand: stone by stone. Shovel
by spadeful like the fireplace
my grandmother built by hand, each
brick set furiously in place. Whatever
contains we let for a thirstier time.
The reserves, our resistance, our resilience,
our certain shelter. All this habitat we give
back, back to the roots of our feet. I
finger tender seedlings back to earth, back
to the grandmother land. All this Earth,
a gift, a homecoming; revival of the species.

## Spring First

Small things make me happy:
fresh garden parsley, organic
everything, the wee ray of light
striking the violet, one shimmer
of a dying sun, still snow in twilight,
blue light on a red lit mountain.
                              Some things
I miss: clods of my earth in my fist,
a wad of paper unfolded to what
I need, someone's handy heart
under my hand, some place to weed
and knead, green valleys of wild mustard,
a remembering face at the gate
when my flight arrives,
                    an arrival.

There are new loves to discover here—
soft coats of moss on the surface of everywhere,
green gateways into fairylands of fir,
the Great Blues loose, wild flying overhead—
their glinting eyes noticing me there; me, here
where I live obstinately loving anew
a new flame—bonfires to come, red clay
in a fiery clearing overhauling time.
                              There is
change—new love to love! There's spring!

## The Farmer in His Dell

*for Bob*


I love that you do
what you say you're going
to do. Strong arms under the guise
of slender wrists. I think I know
you. In all your splendor in the replenished
fields, an acre of extinct seed
brought back to life under your plow.
I pull these sinewed tentacles
from earth. Hear the gun shots
in the distance. A single engine
is tugging a trainload of big leaf
maple, Douglas Fir, new Cherokees,
dense crude oil fracked from the First
Mother. I love how you redeem yourself
over and over, a single reflection, the refracting
of bud, hawk, vine, the hen. As railyards
blow and the chugging wailing trucks
dominate the distance, you shovel decay
into life, sense into sensibilities. You do.

## "Full Moon, Marigolds, Pansies, Tomatoes, Chaya and Mulch"

You're the listmaker, handy
as a pocket on a shirt.
You move about the earth,
a single wave of grass.

In a field ripe with lavender,
lilies and a poppy red sunset
the Buddha Moon beckons. A finger
of potato reaches for marigold.

Under a golden light we spend;
the hearty dirt heaved together in arty
circles. This life we are living into life,
new grown, True Blue as a pansy's mane.

These space blue lions arranged in
symmetry, their heavenly scent abetting
erect heads of sturdy plum tomatoes—
so much the rare green hands, this tropical

transplant chaya. I choose to speak to you
in the conquistador's tongue. But old ways
remain like sticks in the mulch, they'll do.
Dry mushrooms remember, come back

stronger than they were. Love comes
back, a stranger, a blue moon, huger than
it was—I come back to you over and over
in mind like this tilling I can't get enough

of: hardly a season passing and yet
we fuse, graft, thrive, anoint. What's been
before is now as what will come to pass.
This gentle rain. These cold hands. The fire

next time.

## Sudden Song

I could know you.
You gave me half a chance.
Half-wild in the drift of you,
half-child, why wait when the sun
dares the morning? Why wake
when death makes its mark
on a single world gone smaller
and smaller? Still, you smile
an easy grace, a hand's embrace,
awakens. I see you and I know already
always that sudden easy knowing, the way
ghosts among us know. The way is long
or way too short. You are now.
Always already. The Great Divide
awaits. A crow's morning beckons.
A bed and breakfast in the Great
Adventure. It is what it is.
And how it is! This early glistening
is gold—all gravy for the duration.

## Hide

I want to be naked
with your body as my wing
under your unerring rivulets
into your sting. I want to be
flightless, a stone interred,
a hummingbird imbued with Spirit
just come back from your ancient past.
I want to be summer again,
barefoot in the heart of you, your
grass and moss reserve. I want
to be preserved by you, a chorus
of migratory birds in my frothed up
yard, a hunger to touch you, leather
over your wood. Let me be naked
and found again, a discovery. (I could.)
Let me be—skin and heard
and good.

## How Do I Describe the Summer
## With My Eyes Closed?


I'll touch you there
where you keep your small
child's heart, where your sifting
sand plays melodies one can
never hear. I'll raise my
paddles to your wake, make
something unstill for you, shake
you silly, unravel your suit
of mail. I will bask, a solemn
whale or something spurting,
sporting my survival, my bag
of sighs you help me to find.
Here is my pail, let down
your bucket. You will find
me: a crab, a sweetmeat,
a gullible gull in full flight
back to you, an uncharted
country I never left.

# Dogwood

Dogwood blooms in one day
eager for the way Earth
gives up the sun. Prostrate
petals lay, a bee bed, fine
linen sheets, a banquet.

We receive our followers,
hummingbird hosts whirl
around my fake garden skirt.
So much like a love,
all of a sudden: scent
and spray and ray.

My old landlady cut
her dogwood out of season.
Odd twin to the red maple,
neglected with moss and spore
but the heartwood, strong,
febrile passions underfoot.

She wanted another sudden
tree, something exotically expensive,
Heavenly Bamboo or another ornamental
maple. But nothing would grow
in the place of that old stump.
The hardwood taproot, sturdy
where she lay. An angry day,
sap-scent, sawdust spray,
stacked rounds: calves and thighs.

It was just a dogwood.
Just you. In the driver's
seat. You build the road
as we go on. Suddenly, luckily
lost, like my name, a lost
dune in the twilit dusk.

There is a way to go, move,
a reason to this season.
I sink our seed. The Earth
Gives in. I give you the rounds
of burnished wood. The way
you burnish me, smooth me
round. I was in love with
summer. Now spring comes
around and I notice dogwood.

## Sirens of Olympia

Too much of me is can
Aluminum, tin in the river

A waste away orphans are crying
A sea of birds in the sky

Like babies or cats in heat
They cry and cry making the ocean

Sing from the Sound. An inlet
Of prey harbors over them

Reflected as they are in the eternal
This sudden talking of birds

The control of their clasp and letting go
Over the humdrum of traffic

They make raucous mockery of livestock
Again and again the wind strums

A bass—they hate it—let loose
Some search for quarters as some order in

Some are ordered out: The Great
Procession begins overnight

Replaces the echo of birds
Shreds of men hang on the bones

Strung with lights down the avenues
They smell of poverty and sleep

A seabird stutters while madmen eclipse
In the sky by a mimicry of their voices

*Cascadia:* **River Sweet**


*I wish I had a river*
*I could skate away on*

— Joni Mitchell

# River

*for my murdered mother*

I remember the river.
Word you didn't want me
to use. Meaning *Freedom.*
Meaning liberation from the flame.

I remember fire. The lap
of genius dissolving it all,
the light in the dying leaves,
bare fall of it all. I remember.

River of vein in the brain,
the great artery of culture
weaving it together with threads,
conversations. River of immense sorrow.

River of forgiveness. River of the riven
fallen. River of gasping. River of icy
grasp. Fierce river. Fleet river.
Saltless self-revealed in sunlight.

I remember the river: word
you didn't want me to speak. Word,
I free you. Word in your ancient reveal.
The word river, a substitute for desire.

## A Ghazal for Mom

Because you named me Lost I found
Myself. Beside a discovered river I reside.

I flow, I stammer, I love, still, like fish I
Burst from the bubble, my slow residing.

I rise. I expect. I dare. I am a devil—she
To the deceased discoverers, minions who reside.

Here, at the base of all this, all that fighting
Expense, the touch, the bombs, the need to re-side.

Like fish we resurface. We slough off turbulence.
We love like one were the only darling. We reside

Coming on old scales and talons, our shingles
Displayed for all. (There is where we all reside.)

There for love, the final resting for the lost. Lost Land
Of The Deer, is this your final nesting? Do you reside?

## Ode to Philadelphia

Oh, you dirty river turning into nothing!
Unfolding your shallow ribbon of grief,
a vision of nowhere: I see. These were
the moundbuilders, now spirals of gravel
on the way to the mines, the quarries,
the tracks and tracts of distance. Unfolding,
a flatness, the freedom of the range, now
a distant memory. How would it be to ignite,
to set a torch for the victory of the industrial
age, an aging, an ache, a tumor? Winter
persists, stripping the landscape. Coal
shadows of trees line the pits. No birds
stitch the hearts of clouds. The river
reeks, starts over. The wailing of sirens takes
its place. In the silken mudflats, a ripple
of land, a hope.

We emerge like the mighty Mississippi,
a thirst finding its glass, a magnification
on the path to resistance. Here, the hawks fly
free. Eagle sings forgotten rhymes. Rock
made bell, you quell and quench and fill
the banks with more than shredded rumor.
Cached memories subside, a hint, just,
of fish in the blockage. What age is this?
History begins with graphite and ash.
Reminders of ribbons line the presence
now a lack and a fevered fear of fire, the final flood.

Come and try your hand at peace. Make
it ring. Allow destiny to speak (not a girl
on the corner but peace.) Be the change
you want to see: a gathering, glacier slow or crystal
fast. Fast and feed. Drip or storm. It's hurricane
or The Great Relief, a drying out. Inevitable
is just a word some of us heard. It doesn't stick.
Try out and dig. The water's fine, refreshed. (Our
Tears, the blessing of rain.) It's rain or reign or rein.

## Rain and Snow

Fire and water create
a rainbow. Rain and snow
makes slush. Walking away
builds the path. Love
secures the trail.
                    I want
nothing but parted clover,
an open hand at my nape,
a shy dog with his head
in my lap. Neither recreates
the picture outside the frame.
                    I want
nothing but shadows defining,
the edges realigning, nothing
but fog and logs filling
a river, nothing but the boats
loading and unloading. I want to go.
                    I want
no things but feathers,
all the colors in alignment,
all justified columns in
the drifts, an arc of covenance.
I cover you in your seclusion

              a snowy home ago.

## Common Law Knowledge

You can't swim in the same
river twice, but you can build
a raft. You shouldn't burn a bridge
without a boat to sail. The setting
sun only goes once, and then again
before each night. The empty shell
has a life of its own after
the surmise. Startled squirrels
forget their nuts. Every child
sounds the same. Every bird,
different—but same. Ice refreezes.
Steam escapes. All the particles
on the board won't hold a charge
without the bite of saw, the teeth
of time. Wither on the vine doesn't
revive. Water in the lake stays
the same, until it's not.

## River Suite

*at the Garcia Birthday Band Fest*
*"I listen to the river/ sing sweet songs/ to rock my soul."*

A river's dirge:
River says, "slow."
The boats go fast in the NO WAKE
ZONE. The canoers traverse in pairs,
in love or not by proximity. One
lone fisherman in a rubber raft
haunts the belly. Deep water here,
the fish say, SLOW NO WAKE,
a re-sourcing in the mirage
of shallows. Swallows glide, energized.
A stump lives forever for the feeding.
Protecting projects, a wave, a wake
we wake from in the death. One
more murder. Another's investments.
Empty tanks on a slowed horizon.
A full moon rises, unnoticed,
read about in a newsfeed. Pairings
diminish. What is the Soul's Journey
but an empty cabin, molding, or
leaking plastic in the waters our
children's children drink?
Find it in a river. And, think.


Oh, you! A bird wants
to play. Chirping away at Fest,
Tenor for the band!


What poet doesn't love
a river? What fish
Doesn't love the upstream
struggle? Salmon starve
in the tropics. Native souls
drain out in the Northern Great
defrost, a downhill battle.

I carry off this row.
Secure my stitches for the benign
make believe. My Aloysius, a
Hail Mary of sorts. Don't
sort me out. I'm out of school
in my depth. The charge is yours.

Change accepted.


Fished
Fish ripple
In no wake


Five poems on River's
Splendor! Life's lessons learned, and
Then I have to pee.


Dragonfly
Hand big
Came to party


No one sees the bald
Eagle flying over Fest
Aging men dance fast


So many sorrows
Swallowed by the swallows soaring
Through mudflats, larking!


I
Trust you
Dog in boat

*Cascadia:* In Cascadia

## Washington

I'm here now
tracing old paths
through new forests
ancient trees speaking
through their cunning
needle leaves as birds
add and abacus
on the limbs singing
aloud to my soul songs
I feel through the layers
with the souls of my feet
uncover moss-eaten rock
borders of a way into
and not from and line the trails
I am living down to ash
our hearths yield a cold
how garden paths remember

# Haibun: Spring, '17

How many fields are dying? The dead don't care. They come up
in the birds, in the sow's sweet cure, in mums' breath in the twilight,
the sudden sap of star jasmine in the middle of a lonely night.


Night birds punctuate
A lone owl feather falls–soon
It will stay summer

## Unimagined Title

On my murdered mom's
birthday: light rain on expired
seed; new garden, mine.

## Poetry

*"The haiku comes*
*in threes*
*with the virtue of brevity*

*...*

*Thief! Thief!*

*...*

*he'd snatch your life."*
— Robert Hass


The lines come out in fives
and full of change, thick
with their own complications.
I built a spiral coil in dirt
around and around in Dreamtime.

I push through double
time, a half decade of my
life over in a single breath...
I leave through the door of my self—
two stanzas full—the 10 of cups.

# On Feinberg's Theory of Physics

*another for John*

I've always wanted to see these
chevrons live. Far overhead they fly
now, here, in a brave new land of laughing
hydrangeas and rhododendrons, all exotics
in my Garden City of Crossing Rivers confluence.

Here at this black loamy smell of earthworms,
the thick compost, layers of loving, I dive
my hands in, dare to grow. Here, at the feet
of this peeling rock, the distinct pillars of red
stone slab, an ancient clay awaits the hand.

My deep brown hands, the palms smooth
this Good Friday day, no ashen cross residual
of sorrow on my head, but there. Nonetheless
what is, now: the dear, the winsome almost
there, the wee particular particles of a life

well-lived, my own. Here, where a hard life
meets some weak interactions, the crossed
graphs of loving, all those might-have-beens,
the now no more—but memory: the unexpressed,
inexpressible force. Here, in this random matrix

I face the final (?) summation of my single missing
ring, what is not thrown away by that beloved
someone else—so long ago—the not-so-well-
loved loved well. I loved him, a self in-so-spectral
introspection; a certainty. This I know, non-hermetic,

the local and delocalized. I walk about this de-
localization, circling aimlessly around some
nowhere no one's planet loneliness. I give
into it: that dream of super symmetry, some
lost quantum for a static bag. It's a learning

curve, I see. I tell myself. Fifty years of sudden
never-change, the only constant. It's you
or you or you or no one solid. All is fluid, a

renormalizing affect. The kinks and bounds
just another way to say: I miss you, in all

this decay, my coherent collision, your too
short wave, an essential singularity to a finite
order of one. Here, is it the end of a life I am
beginning? Come and cross me. Dot my eyes. I,
so damp at the theory of you, my never known

factor, some irreducible matter: my amplitude.
My one...

## Out The Window and Into the Fall,
## San Francisco, 2012


My neighbor's aspen is dying.
The few gingko here succumb
to bulldozers and drought.
Ancient enough to have fed
the dinosaurs, they resist
into winter, let their foul fruit fly,
litter the campuses and sticky
the labels.
           I dwell
past the past with its past
teeth biting bad dreams; a rabid dog
passes. I let it. I let
in the wind. It clears
the urine smell of my "new"
apartment. One black cat, watching
the white moth flicker, its mouth
ravaged by rats. The Mexican (Mayan?)
busboy shutters the back storage units
as the hungry feline spies live birds
loitering in the withered leaves the color
of slabs of rock I left behind.
                Here,
in this weathering season, the crouching
cat crouches while crows crow and mice
and men wait for some other sign;
soon the chainsaws will arrive.

## Dogwood (Two)

A heart turned upside down
is empty, a wooden chair
without. Carved intricacies
all aflare, unnoticed there;
a dogwood chair, its lovers
gone under. Who needs a foyer
without a home? Who needs
a pause to remember the boot
one doesn't walk in? A bargain
boast, there for the discovery.
By chance a chance to buy
something that lasts. It won't be
long there. The hills are full
of coupling. The motors go.
The guns go off. The postal
flags, ablaze this sudden
summer season. Half a day
already casts its shadow,
a pregnant profile, fireworks
in one day—all the bees, a buzzing.
A flower turns to something.

## Mayflies Mating

Oh, you opposing dancers!
Locked in your lust magnets,
a single linked desire,
                  I desire
you, the want of you.
Your hungry ant disguise
fools the eye—at first.
At once you tug and pull,
push into dragonfly status.
All your will, a willing trance,
a stop-time dance, stallion's
prance. I salute you, hardy
hearty fliers protecting my garden,
resisting extinction. Imago
past-nymph primitives,
                  I honor
you, your love-stance circumstance,
a winsome unit of measure and
message: "Semper Fi!"

## Dance Me to the End of Love

*for Billie*


There's motorboat play on Green Lake.
I can hear them grunting and grasping.
Shards of sparkle devastate a reflection
of fronded pool, the calm down under.

I come to this willow to soke
my rock. The sulking mammals penetrate.
All my life I've driven here, a destination
unbound. Unwound, I see.

The bastions of dazzle, woven yards
of friends like Berber rugs; the pedigree,
the young, the fine divide intrinsic
to this stance: this bridal spray

and dance. In the wake: fine lines
before the rustled diamonds ray, a horizon
of fluttering, a rehoming; the cloud massed banks,
still green expanse, the endless traffic back.

## When Blue Herons Come

When blue herons come home
to roost, when swallows refuse
to return, when the last bird settles
the score on a ripped up lake, when still
water stills into something else

I'll be stolid as an apartment
complex, sly as a sliding door,
enamored of nothing but. But
the fading of the light sparks the end
of twilight shy light expanding and

a something else introduces itself
upon the horizon: the blush of split
salmon, ash of dusk, some huge
mammalian presence shaping into
killer whale before me. Nothing but

the ripple of children, laughing.

## Seattle Seance

*for Alfred Arteaga*


An old ghost of a love
led me here by heart, stroked
my rump unsalaciously, caressingly,
but clear as day in the day,
a clear signal from a ghost
who loved me. I couldn't feel
that Spirit, but knowing, hearing
words he'd written. Clearly. (In his voice!)

A ghost. The dead speak in ways
only an animal within us sages.
They stay in bars, linger at bus
stops, stroke the butts of those
who really loved them as they garden.
I look away. I see you texting another
(your goofy heartbreaking grin), a smile eager
at what's before you. I pull your weeds

in another woman's garden (wife?)
with a wedding to plan, bouquets
to envision…. Touched by a ghost, summoned;
I ask: What are you doing? "Music research."
"This book I'm reading." (Same as hers?)
"I've been touched by a ghost." "Caressed
my left butt cheek, lovingly." (I heard it say,
*There's a lot you have to learn about men.)*
                              So I looked.

In the morning I was single.

## Poem For Many Colors

That morning you fished a salmon
from that urban river and carried
it back by the gills in front of the stunned
tourists—its tail scraping the pavement as you
tramped—big beautiful guy that you were...

That didn't make up for it.

Or that night you carved me
a rainbow or painted my carved
cedar goddess with acrylic without asking;
or the day you chased and caught me,
the etched half-moon in your eye...

That didn't make up for it.

Nor the too hot afternoon you took me
up the burning scramble telling me tales
of wild lions big as a train car, *snout to tail,*
and forced me to eat cheese as the mountain
would hurt me more *being bigger...*

That didn't make up for it.

Nor the three nights I spent making
your art (your manic hands, your hindered
heart). (You taught me how to carve.) You taught
me to whittle the weakness away. You led
me to see—the unexpected, the shoe, the wallet...

That didn't make up for it.

You taught me a single word: *Menesenora,*
Many Colors, your father's father's father's name;
how to never wash a plate (press the espinas, thorns
together, and wait.) You taught me to catch fish, stunned
by the oxygen of it all, at the waterfall, stupid at hand...

And that didn't make up for it.

## Dancing With Roethke

*for The Blue Moon Tavern*

> *"We sing together; we sing mouth to mouth.*
> *The garden is a river flowing south.*
> *She cries out loud the soul's own secret joy;*
> *She dances, and the ground bears her away.*
> *She knows the speech of light, and makes it plain*
> *A lively thing can come to life again."*
> — Theodore Roethke from "She"


They came to jizz, to jazz
and fizz, to toot their horns. They did.
Clever women, unsung sheroes, wits
like gifts of seedlings in the pot, plucked
out, or triumphed. Between the bass notes,
the rows of writhing dancers, twirls of sass.
Brass and Black soldiers home
from war. Finally. Home. Langston,
home. While outside, the vivid
lightning strikes. Big men drank here.
Diamond women "lovely in their bones."
They filled their aching hearts with
booze, with needle looks, with fair
dominion. They lost their fairy lives
to it. Ted. Dick. Dylan... Wonderful
women broke a bottle here to launch
them. Here's to you, Carolyn. It's gin
and a tonic to absence. Allen, swaying
to his angelic harmonium, saying, "Fuck
you!" to Ken. (It could have happened
here.) Bill. David... Stanley, the man
who taught the poets' sacred task — the work
that fills you with empty. I raise my glass,
my one, to you, Ted. Not even Cassady
could hold a candle. Jack drank
to it all his too short wick. Big
dreams dreamed here, between the beats,
the back bar benches, the snowy moon
breaks. Another generation fans
out: the brilliant, the bold, the band —
the movers of the Spirit that moves us here

to steal your face. It isn't far
from the greenhouse to the bar.
But somehow they'll save us all
(with grace.)

Poem In the Time of Rain

   *for Greta and Water Protector, Autumn Peltier*

   *"When you produce peace,*
   *you project peace."*

   *"...we're going for the stars!"*
      *—Nassim Haramein, physicist*


Any body can prosper
peace who makes it.

After rain, the doves
fly out, swallows soar

and do it for dirt
and water. The mud

bricks of our walls
and hovels crumble.

Everywhere, matter!
The fine leavings

of our love surprise
hold it to a quarter

of time past. The future,
unbelievable. Thick by

thick we construct
our story while the thin

grease of the living and
dying fills us with mercy.

It's tough work to hoe.
It's a hard world but some

one will save her.

## Delphi Deux

Harvest time has come full-throttled
and gone in time. This rare and brilliant
winter; that unusual spring with its thrush
in hiding in the dying big leaf maples. Cedar
bursts into flying flames, brittle on the owl's
branch, now a woodpecker's workshop,
while a displaced squirrel raves above
the sound of chainsaws and the neighbors'
automatic weaponry, the rave of buzzing
Hawk helicopters bound for duty and the buzzless
stinging wasps. All was well... until it's not.
Roots rot beneath the stumps. Timber bound
for someone's countertop. While good earth
stands abandoned... fruits of love I do not harvest.

## For It

You gave me moss
in winter. You gave me
trilliums and the name

for it. You gave me summer
in a tame hornets nest.
You gave me autumn

in an ancient squash,
in my favorite cocklike
cornstalk, and a place

for it. You gave me spring
time in the haunting
thrush's cry. You gave

me my place in the sun
until the shadows fell,
until moon made a dare

for it. You gave me
rock and the welt
of wood, the weft

of fine grain, the pull
and twist, the spit
and fire finish of it

for It.

## Soul I Say

I will teach you the other thunder,
ash music of waving praise, the dark
need of the chiming would. People chew
bread, load praise on an altar of brown
rice and red beans, an ancient worship.

I will build you my nation in an egg,
sour burned roses, the Alabanza
of frogs on overtime. Dial in
my bristles, the night burst
dam where I dance, floating.

Even my shoulder mingles
with the praises of pirates.
Chant. Crack. Name. Squint
and you can almost see the sails
above the city's tattoo of striking.

My harbor of quakes awakes, my faceless
Soul where diminutive mouths of empty
sacks praise my lack. The sea, that other
god, a shudder, a tree, the ocean
where my last lost restaurant waits.

# PRAISE FOR LORNA DEE CERVANTES' APRIL ON OLYMPIA

From the first poem, "The River Doesn't Want the Wall," my heart skipped a beat. Cervantes hurriedly invites the reader into the river current of her words with a community call: "The river wants to let freedom ring!" In this much anticipated collection of poems, Lorna Dee Cervantes writes truth to the "post-nuclear age" with grace and poignancy. She is truly a prophetic voice for these times. —Brenda Vaca

In *April on Olympia*, Lorna Dee Cervantes wagers that love is a force greater than fear. This is no paean to positive thinking. *April in Olympia* is love as rough- hewn landscape, as that which is truly a force. These are poems of great and needful praise, and equally needful damnation. This book has beautiful and vital ferocity. No wall could withstand the surging river of these poems. —Joe Weil

Covering topics as diverse as nature and the environment; war and politics; relationships and aging; dancing and music– and spanning a time frame of nearly fifty years – the collection reminds us of our interconnectedness with one another and the earth, the planet we all share. —America Hart

*April on Olympia* has something for everyone. In "Destination Anywhere" (after Allen Ginsberg), a personal favorite in this collection, Cervantes' driving poetic lines, complemented by her deft application of vivid images, confront the horrors of a 21st century and its "heart of darkness" corollary with memorable passion, precision, and grit. —Sterling Warner

In her true cultural-warrior style, esta guerrera prompts us to pay tribute to our teachers, to be conscious of the pleasure of being, simply being. Bien hecho, hermana. Adelante! —Irene I. Blea

Now, I get to say that I have fallen in love with the work of Lorna Dee Cervantes.... "It's Not The Tulips' Fault" knits the history of tulips as commodity to the migrant work related to their production in a long, image-dense poem that reinforces the immense impact of a single crop on a people. —Miriam O'Neil

Lorna Dee Cervantes' poem,"'What Is XicanX?'" reminds the reader that she is the revolutionary chick from the beat poets. Her poems are meant to be heard. You have to read them aloud to hear her message, and it's a strong one. She says get off your ass and change the world. Now, pendejo, now. —Juliana Aragón Fatula

Lorna Dee Cervantes is a XicanIndx (Chumash/Purepacha) author of five award-winning books of poetry: Emplumada (Pitt Poetry Series 1981); From the Cables of Genocide: Poems on Love and Hunger (Arte Publico Press 1991); Ciento: 100 100-Word Love Poems (Wings Press 2011); Drive: The First Quartet (Wings Press 2005); and Sueño (Wings Press 2013). The founder of MANGO Publications (first to publish Sandra Cisneros), Cervantes is also the recipient of two NEA grants, two Pushcart Prizes, a Lila Wallace Readers Digest grant, and three state arts poetry fellowships. She presented twice at the Library of Congress as well as hundreds of universities, colleges and other venues. The former Director of Creative Writing at CU Boulder, where she was a professor for 20 years, she up and moved to Olympia, WA in 2014, and now lives and writes in Seattle.

# Titles From Marsh Hawk Press

Jane Augustine *Arbor Vitae; Krazy; Night Lights; A Woman's Guide to Mountain Climbing*

Tom Beckett *Dipstick (Diptych)*

Sigman Byrd *Under the Wanderer's Star*

Patricia Carlin: *Original Green; Quantum Jitters; Second Nature*

Claudia Carlson *The Elephant House; My Chocolate Sarcophagus; Pocket Park*

Lorna Dee Cervantes: *April on Olympia*

Meredith Cole *Miniatures*

Jon Curley *Hybrid Moments; Scorch Marks; Remnant Halo*

Neil de la Flor *Almost Dorothy; An Elephant's Memory of Blizzards*

Chard deNiord *Sharp Golden Thorn*

Sharon Dolin *Serious Pink*

Steve Fellner *Blind Date with Cavafy; The Weary World Rejoices*

Thomas Fink *Selected Poems & Poetic Series; Joyride; Peace Conference; Clarity and Other Poems; After Taxes; Gossip*

Thomas Fink and Maya D. Mason *A Pageant for Every Addiction*

Norman Finkelstein *Inside the Ghost Factory; Passing Over*

Edward Foster *A Looking-Glass for Traytors; The Beginning of Sorrows; Dire Straits; Mahrem: Things Men Should Do for Men; Sewing the Wind; What He Ought to Know*

Paolo Javier *The Feeling is Actual*

Burt Kimmelman *Abandoned Angel; Somehow*

Burt Kimmelman and Fred Caruso *The Pond at Cape May Point*

Basil King *Disparate Beasts: Basil King's Beastiary, Part Two; 77 Beasts; Disparate Beasts; Mirage; The Spoken Word / The Painted Hand from Learning to Draw / A History*

Martha King *Imperfect Fit*

Phillip Lopate *At the End of the Day: Selected Poems and An Introductory Essay*

Mary Mackey *Breaking the Fever; The Jaguars That Prowl Our Dreams; Sugar Zone; Travelers With No Ticket Home*

Jason McCall *Dear Hero,*

Sandy McIntosh *The After-Death History of My Mother; Between Earth and Sky; Cemetery Chess; Ernesta, in the Style of the Flamenco; Forty-Nine Guaranteed Ways to Escape Death; A Hole In the Ocean; Lesser Lights; Obsessional*

Stephen Paul Miller *Any Lie You Tell Will Be the Truth; The Bee Flies in May; Fort Dad; Skinny Eighth Avenue; There's Only One God and You're Not It*

Daniel Morris *Blue Poles; Bryce Passage; Hit Play; If Not for the Courage*

Gail Newman *Blood Memory*

Geoffrey O'Brien *Where Did Poetry Come From; The Blue Hill*

Sharon Olinka *The Good City*

Christina Olivares *No Map of the Earth Includes Stars*

Justin Petropoulos *Eminent Domain*

Paul Pines *Charlotte Songs; Divine Madness; Gathering Sparks; Last Call at the Tin Palace*

Jacquelyn Pope *Watermark*

George Quasha *Things Done for Themselves*

Karin Randolph *Either She Was*

Rochelle Ratner *Balancing Acts; Ben Casey Days; House and Home*

Michael Rerick *In Ways Impossible to Fold*

Corrine Robins *Facing It; One Thousand Years; Today's Menu*

Eileen R. Tabios *The Connoisseur of Alleys; I Take Thee, English, for My Beloved; The In(ter)vention of the Hay(na)ku; The Light Sang as It Left Your Eyes; Reproductions of the Empty Flagpole; Sun Stigmata; The Thorn Rosary*

Eileen R. Tabios and j/j hastain *The Relational Elations of Orphaned Algebra*

Tony Trigilio: *Proof Something Happened*

Susan Terris *Familiar Tense; Ghost of Yesterday; Natural Defenses*

Lynne Thompson *Fretwork*

Madeline Tiger *Birds of Sorrow and Joy*

Tana Jean Welch *Latest Volcano*

Harriet Zinnes: *Drawing on the Wall; Light Light or the Curvature of the Earth; New and Selected Poems; Weather is Whether; Whither Nonstopping*

| YEAR | AUTHOR | TITLE | JUDGE |
|---|---|---|---|
| 2004 | Jacquelyn Pope | *Watermark* | Marie Ponsot |
| 2005 | Sigman Byrd | *Under the Wanderer's Star* | Gerald Stern |
| 2006 | Steve Fellner | *Blind Date with Cavafy* | Denise Duhamel |
| 2007 | Karin Randolph | *Either She Was* | David Shapiro |
| 2008 | Michael Rerick | *In Ways Impossible to Fold* | Thylias Moss |
| 2009 | Neil de la Flor | *Almost Dorothy* | Forrest Gander |
| 2010 | Justin Petropoulos | *Eminent Domain* | Anne Waldman |
| 2011 | Meredith Cole | *Miniatures* | Alicia Ostriker |
| 2012 | Jason McCall | *Dear Hero,* | Cornelius Eady |
| 2013 | Tom Beckett | *Dipstick (Diptych)* | Charles Bernstein |
| 2014 | Christina Olivares | *No Map of the Earth Includes Stars* | Brenda Hillman |
| 2015 | Tana Jean Welch | *Latest Volcano* | Stephanie Strickland |
| 2016 | Robert Gibb | *After* | Mark Doty |
| 2017 | Geoffrey O'Brien | *The Blue Hill* | Meena Alexander |
| 2018 | Lynne Thompson | *Fretwork* | Jane Hirshfield |
| 2019 | Gail Newman | *Blood Memory* | Marge Piercy |
| 2020 | Tony Trigilio | *Proof Something Happened* | Susan Howe |
| 2021 | Joanne D. Dwyer | *Rasa* | David Lehman |